Home is
the Hurt is

Domestic Violence
and the Church's Response

by
Rosie Nixson

Curate, St Andrew's, Hartcliffe, Bristol

GROVE BOOKS LIMITED
Bramcote Nottingham NG9 3DS

Contents

Introduction 3
1. 'It Doesn't Happen Round Here…' 4
    What is Domestic Violence? 4
    Statistics 5
    Violence against Women of the Church Community 6
2. 'A Sin and a Crime'? 7
    Contemporary Approaches: Causes 7
    Cultural Issues 11
    Practical Responses 12
3. 'Battered into Submission'? 14
    Theological Issues 14
    Interpreting the Bible 15
    Church History and Tradition 17
    The Church Today 17
4. Loosing the Chains of Injustice 19
    Pastoral Responses 19
    Challenges for the Church 22
Further Reading 24

Copyright Rosie Nixson 1994

ACKNOWLEDGEMENTS

I would like to thank the many people who have contributed to this booklet by answering letters, being interviewed, pointing me to written resources, and sharing their experiences.

'Power and control' and 'Equality' diagrams reproduced with permission from the Domestic Abuse Intervention Project, 206 West Fourth Street, Duluth, Minnesota 55806, USA.

The Cover Picture is by Tiffany Ponsonby

First Impression June 1994
ISSN 0144-171X
ISBN 1 85174 269 7

Introduction

'My nightmare began. Why? I haven't a clue
He just stopped my housekeeping, out of the blue
Then came, "You're so ugly, so stupid, a spendthrift, a tart"
And those profound words of wisdom were only the start.
And for years, an endless dark nightmare of years
I cried with no tears.

He progressed to kicking, raping, starving and blacking my eyes
And when I sought help they believed him, it was all lies
I became ill, and depressed, lonely for love
I begged the Lord for deliverance
Please, I cried, take the violence from his eyes—
   it's evil and malevolent
Yet for more years, an endless dark nightmare of years
I cried with no tears.'[1]

I will never forget one evening in my home group. It started as an ordinary Bible study. But suddenly, Mary, a fairly new member, broke down. Her husband regularly beat or abused her. She couldn't leave him because she was economically dependent. We were the first people she'd ever told.

'The Church', in the person of the group leader, now had to respond, but generally the issue seems hardly on our agenda. The challenge to place it there was made in *Faith in the City*, with an observation that rigid views of the family are unhelpful, Christian perspectives of male dominance and female subservience might contribute to an atmosphere where abuse was tolerated, and clergy needed to consider advice other than urging women to put up with the suffering. There was also a call to support local initiatives such as women's refuges, and some practical guidelines on how to help 'battered wives'. However, little seems to have happened. An ordinand at one college could almost be forgiven for responding to some questions of mine on the subject, 'It's not something pastors generally have to deal with'.

Why is there so little awareness? In the last few years, public awareness of domestic violence has increased considerably. Perhaps for many church people, domestic violence, if they are aware of it at all, is a 'private issue'. Or it is seen as a 'women's issue'—and the fact that often the only campaigners have been seen as radical feminists has not helped. Or perhaps it is too 'political', not something the church should be concerned about. And churches do not like to admit the existence of family violence, in a context

---

[1] Quoted in L Macdonald, 'Women, religion and violence', *Life and Work*.

where 'family' is so central.

Furthermore, one major contributory factor in domestic violence, according to recent secular and Christian literature, is the teaching of the church. To question long-standing Christian teaching is threatening. Some of those currently questioning it are outside the mainstream of the church, so not likely to be listened to.

And finally, the issue is not just domestic violence in society, it is domestic violence in Christian homes. And that is a thoroughly uncomfortable thought.

Those who are most aware of the problem are sometimes suspicious of Christians. We ourselves, convinced of the liberating power of the gospel, may be tempted to suggest easy answers. Most church people know little about domestic violence, and this booklet aims to provide some basic information and insight, before suggesting the challenge of some theological issues, and some ways in which Church leaders and members might respond to this neglected and disturbing issue. If the claim that Jesus came to bring life in all its fulness means anything, we have a responsibility to bring the message of that life to all people—and especially those whose hope in life has all but died.

1
'It Doesn't Happen Round Here...'

What is Domestic Violence?

Domestic violence is threatened, attempted or actual violence by a partner or ex-partner, i.e. within or after a relationship of marriage or cohabitation. It is essentially the misuse of power and the exercise of control by one person, usually the man, over another, usually the woman. There are a small number of instances of violence against men by women, but domestic violence generally refers to violence against women from known men. Violence in the home can also involve violence to children, but that is really another large area, and will not be covered in this booklet.

There are quite a few myths about domestic violence—that it only happens in 'problem' or working class families, that the men who use violence come from violent backgrounds, that alcohol is to blame, that it's not that serious. The myths need to be dispelled.

'Battered women come from all walks of life. Social class, family income, level of education, occupation, and ethnic or racial background make no difference.'[1]

'Olive—was raped by her husband
Gwen—was humiliated in front of her friends
Liz—was slapped when the meal was not ready
Shaneem—was often locked out
Sandra—was kicked downstairs
Janet—was abused and insulted'[2]

Abuse can be physical, sexual, or psychological. If violence happens once, it is likely to happen often. It escalates in frequency and intensity over time. The following are just a few examples.

'He knocked me out, my face was bruised and all out of proportion. He bruised my back and spine and I sprained a wrist. My body was all marked by this whipping with a metal spring belt. He pulled half the hair in my head out, my mouth was bleeding and I lost a tooth. I had a black eye and split bleeding lips.'[3]

'..anytime things went wrong at the office, I'd take it out at home. I could always find something to go off my head about, bikes on the drive, anything. It'd be, "Can't you keep your bloody kids under control!" She'd go berserk at the kids, really lay into them, and I would sit there satisfied, reading the paper, in total control...'.[4]

'Once he threw a radio at me. It bounced off the wall and smashed my skull open. I had to have 32 stitches. He was angry about something at work, I was trying to calm him down and he saw that as taking someone else's side. He poured paint all over my hair because he didn't like the way I had it cut. He'd tell me what to wear, how to vote, where to work; I had no control at all.'

This does not make pleasant reading. But it must be said, because it is only by recognising that such violence is a serious injustice that we can begin to think out our response to it. Just as the church has recently begun to consider issues such as sexual abuse and rape, it must face the existence of this violence, thousands of women living in fear, shame and misery.

Statistics

Domestic violence is a worldwide phenomenon. But as it is probably the most unreported crime, statistics are hard to come by. One study in Scotland found that less than 3% of all physical attacks by husbands and other males on women in the household were reported to the police.[5] So if 25% of all recorded violent crime is wife assault, it is likely the unrecorded instances

1 Lorna J F Smith, 1989, *Domestic Violence*, London: HMSO. p 16.
2 WAFE leaflet, 'What is Women's Aid?'
3 Quoted Smith, p 17.
4 P Stirling, 1992, 'Stop the Bashings', *Listener*, (New Zealand) June 22 1992, p 22.
5 J Hanmer, 1983, *Violence against Women*, Milton Keynes: Open University Press, p 16.

would make this much higher.[1]

It has been estimated that about one in four marriages or partnerships experience physical violence at some point.[2] That must be a fair few in every parish.

Estimates suggest that there are three quarters of a million domestic violence incidents in London per year (London Strategic Policy Unit 1986). Research conducted in 1989 for Hammersmith and Fulham Council found that 48% of women experienced verbal or physical threats from a household member or male partner; 30% of women have been physically assaulted at least once.

Data on grounds for divorce suggest that in 1980 as many as 45,000 marriages in England and Wales were ended as a result of violence by husbands against their wives.[3]

Violence against Women of the Church Community

A report by the Presbyterian church in New Zealand identifies members of the church as both abusers and abused. There is evidence that women in the church are beaten by their husbands—some of whom are clergy.

An American pastor, Kenneth Petersen, has documented wife abuse in Christian families in the US, as have James and Phyllis Alsdurf, authors of *Battered into Submission*. The Alsdurfs cite extensive research and summarise eight years of interviews with abused, abusers and pastors. Some pastors blamed women for not being submissive enough to their husbands' rightful dominance. Counsel often focused on keeping the family together, regardless of the violence.

Many women have found that leaving an abusive spouse meant leaving the church. *Keeping the Faith*, a booklet by an American minister, Marie Fortune, was written for Christian women who have been battered, helping them to retain faith and trust in God.

In Britain, evidence of wife abuse within Christian families has been uncovered, but little has been written on the subject. In 1989 a retired vicar bludgeoned his wife to death over two hours when he had trouble with radio reception. He had previously beaten his wife during their long marriage. The publication of an article in the *Independent* by Elaine Storkey, on wife abuse within 'Christian' families, resulted in callous media interest. Not surprisingly, the women concerned retreated into silence, having also discovered that the church did not want to know.[4]

Domestic violence is a pervasive problem in society, and a problem within the church too.

---

1 Hanmer, p 17.
2 Smith, p 14; G Hague and E Malos, 1993, *Domestic Violence*, p 12.
3 Smith, p 13.
4 E Storkey, 'Abused twice over', *Third Way*, November 1988, p 8.

2
'A Sin and a Crime'?

Domestic violence may seem to be a new 'problem'. But where has it come from? How has it arisen? And what are the causes of this violence? Before we look at contemporary understanding, a glance at history. It seems there is a long, legal, church-sanctioned, tradition of wife beating, part of the right of a husband in an unequal marriage relationship. Augustine, writing on marriage, affirmed that 'woman ought to serve her husband as unto God, affirming that in no thing hath woman equal power as unto God, affirming that woman ought to be repressed'. The Council of Toledo in AD 400 declared: 'A husband is bound to chastise his wife moderately, unless he be a cleric, in which case he may chastise her harder.'

The sixteenth century Spanish humanist Luis Vives, in his *Instruccion de la mujer cristiana*, assumes the essential inferiority of woman and advises submission to her husband: 'If he lays hands on you for some fault of yours or in a fit of madness, imagine that it is God who is punishing you, and that this is happening because of your sins, and that in this way you are doing penance for them. You are fortunate if, with a little suffering in this life, you gain remission of the torments of the next. In fact, very few good and prudent women are beaten by their husbands, however bad and mad they may be....'[1]

In Thomas More's picture of an ideal society, 'husbands are pictured as chastising their wives, the wives as ministering to their husbands in all things, falling prostrate at their feet on holy days, and asking their forgiveness if they have offended them in any way.'[2] A couple of sayings illustrate the tradition: 'A woman, a spaniel and a walnut tree, the more they are beaten, the better they be' (c 1600). 'Our women are like dogs, the more you beat them, the better they love you' (nineteenth century).

In 1782 a judge ruled that a man could beat his wife if the stick was no thicker than his thumb. Until 1861 it was legal to beat your wife before dusk, after which it might disturb the neighbours. This became a criminal offence under the Offences against the Person Act. In 1891 the legal right of the English husband to restrain his wife by physical means was completely abolished. However, the tradition seems to have remained.

Contemporary Approaches: Causes

Before 1970 there was little serious writing on men's violence to women. As women's centres were set up in the early 70s, women began to share their

---

1   Quoted in *Concilium* 1994/1, p 102.
2   J C Brown and C R Bohm (ed.), 1989, *Christianity, Patriarchy and Abuse*, Cleveland: The Pilgrim Press, p 35.

experiences; and around the same time the issue was 'discovered' by professionals—academics and social scientists. With the rise of feminism, women who had been abused started to write about it. Erin Pizzey's *Scream Quietly or the Neighbours Will Hear* (1974) brought the issue to the attention of many people for the first time.

The first refuge in the world was opened in Chiswick in 1972, and since then thousands have come into existence. A national agency in England (now Women's Aid Federation England, abbreviated to WAFE) was established in 1975 by 35 groups which were running or establishing refuges, and remains the most influential organisation.

Writing has been confined mainly to academic or feminist publications, and a variety of explanations have been proposed for the causes of men's violence to women. The most fundamental question is: is the aggressor or the victim to blame?

The first, psychopathological theories, sought to account for men's violence by seeing it as the result of some inherent aberration or abnormality. Batterers are psychotics or psychopaths. Such views still persist to some extent.

From the 70s victim-blaming theories became popular. These viewed women as in some way 'asking for it'. Freudian theories of female masochism supported this, and writers like Pizzey, who posited the idea of 'violence-prone' women (i.e. women who grew up in abusive families, became addicted to violence, and sought out violent partners) perpetuated it. It has been much criticized for ignoring social and cultural influences, though it continues to be influential in the USA.

The idea that the woman is to blame is widely held, however. One woman described the most recent occasion her public-school educated 'model' husband had hit her, giving her a black eye and bruising. He said she deserved it, because she was so incompetent, and he was so wonderful. Feeling suicidal, she had talked of taking her own life, and he suggested she'd be doing the world a favour. When in her distress she had told her parents, their response was that if her husband had hit her, she must have deserved it.

Other psychological theories see a causal relationship between violence and the effects of alcohol. Men who are violent to their partners have sometimes been drinking. Alcohol may accompany violence, but the root cause of the violence lies elsewhere.

Another major psychological theory, that of learned helplessness, was developed by Lenore Walker. Women have discovered they are unable to stop the beatings and have therefore learned helplessness. This view has been criticized because it pathologizes the woman and means that woman who try to stand up to the violence are not seem as real victims.

There are various sociological theories which contribute insight on how violence is learned behaviour or a reaction to stressful external factors. But these tend to blame the women or the environment and avoid looking at men's personal responsibility. Finally, two of the most influential academics on this subject, Dobash and Dobash, look at social construction: institutional sexism supports men's violence to women.

There have been several attempts to analyse what happens around a violent incident. The first such model was a 'cycle of violence', developed by Lenore Walker.

The cycle has three phases, Tension-building, Battering, Regret and Respite. Some trigger leads to violence, then there is calm, and regret. Women often say, 'He promised it would never happen again'. But usually the cycle continues, and if uninterrupted, generally becomes faster and more violent.

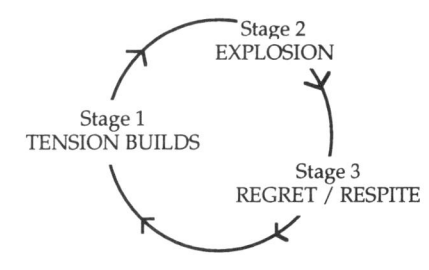

Stage 1 TENSION BUILDS
Stage 2 EXPLOSION
Stage 3 REGRET / RESPITE

This cycle seemed rather too simple, and an amended cycle of violence was devised by two men involved in developing programmes for men who are violent to women.[1] This isolates four decision points at the first stage. First, the man does not recognise that tension is building. He withdraws, or escapes into work. Then by 'labelling' he reduces the woman to an object of lesser importance, rather than an equal human being. He may call her a bitch, a slag, a slut, a slob, or emotional, hysterical, frigid, ugly, etc. He carries on, and follows her around, and perhaps ends by cornering her, and hitting her.

The final decision, to use physical violence, may occur when the woman seems to defy the man, or refuse a service that is expected. In the earlier example, a woman had a radio thrown at her when she was perceived to be taking sides against her husband. This is the moment of crisis. Another woman, pinned to the wall with her feet off the ground and her partner's hands around her throat, feared she was about to die.

The cycle may not always end with violence, if control is achieved by name-calling or threatening and intimidating behaviour.

However, the whole cycle model, which has been quite influential, is limited. It fits the experience of some women, but does not cover the range of abusive behaviours and attitudes which women encounter. For example, one man who hit his wife because of her 'incompetence' showed no remorse at all. Rather than saying sorry afterwards, he just said she deserved everything she got.

Recent writings by women, WAFE and other agencies focus on culture

---

1   K McMaster & P Swain, 1989, *A Private Affair?* Wellington: GP Books.

and social construction as the origin of domestic violence, and centre on issues of power and control. The power and control model is now widely used to understand abuse. Men use power and control in a variety of ways. A man may establish and maintain control with a combination of charm and cruelty. If he is violent and apologises, the woman is likely to assume it is an isolated incident. He may become gradually more controlling, restricting her activities and her contact with friends and family. The woman wants the violence to stop, but becomes increasingly powerless to act, and feels dehumanized and demoralized, so it may take her a long time to tell anyone, or consider leaving.

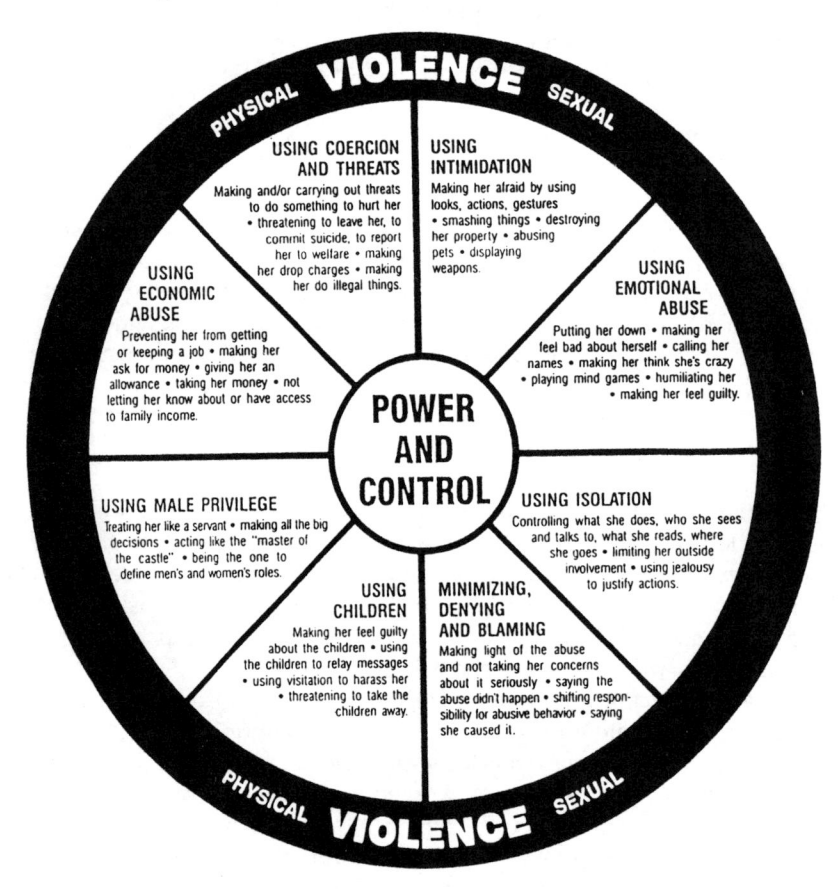

PHYSICAL VIOLENCE SEXUAL

POWER AND CONTROL

USING COERCION AND THREATS
Making and/or carrying out threats to do something to hurt her • threatening to leave her, to commit suicide, to report her to welfare • making her drop charges • making her do illegal things.

USING INTIMIDATION
Making her afraid by using looks, actions, gestures • smashing things • destroying her property • abusing pets • displaying weapons.

USING EMOTIONAL ABUSE
Putting her down • making her feel bad about herself • calling her names • making her think she's crazy • playing mind games • humiliating her • making her feel guilty.

USING ISOLATION
Controlling what she does, who she sees and talks to, what she reads, where she goes • limiting her outside involvement • using jealousy to justify actions.

MINIMIZING, DENYING AND BLAMING
Making light of the abuse and not taking her concerns about it seriously • saying the abuse didn't happen • shifting responsibility for abusive behavior • saying she caused it.

USING CHILDREN
Making her feel guilty about the children • using the children to relay messages • using visitation to harass her • threatening to take the children away.

USING MALE PRIVILEGE
Treating her like a servant • making all the big decisions • acting like the "master of the castle" • being the one to define men's and women's roles.

USING ECONOMIC ABUSE
Preventing her from getting or keeping a job • making her ask for money • giving her an allowance • taking her money • not letting her know about or have access to family income.

PHYSICAL VIOLENCE SEXUAL

The opposite of power is equality, which will result in non-controlling attitudes and non violent behaviour. The power and control model has been expressed in diagram form by the Domestic Abuse Intervention Project in Duluth, Minnesota.

In this model, the 'equality' wheel seems to reflect the kind of radical equality between men and women which Christ sought to restore. Also, men's personal responsibility is seen as crucial. This obviously comes closer to the kind of perspective which Christians might want to take. Socialization is part of the problem—hence a challenge to change thinking. But if sin is an essential part of the human condition, then sin must be recognised as such. Thus concepts of guilt and responsibility are also central, so repentance and forgiveness can become part of the solution.

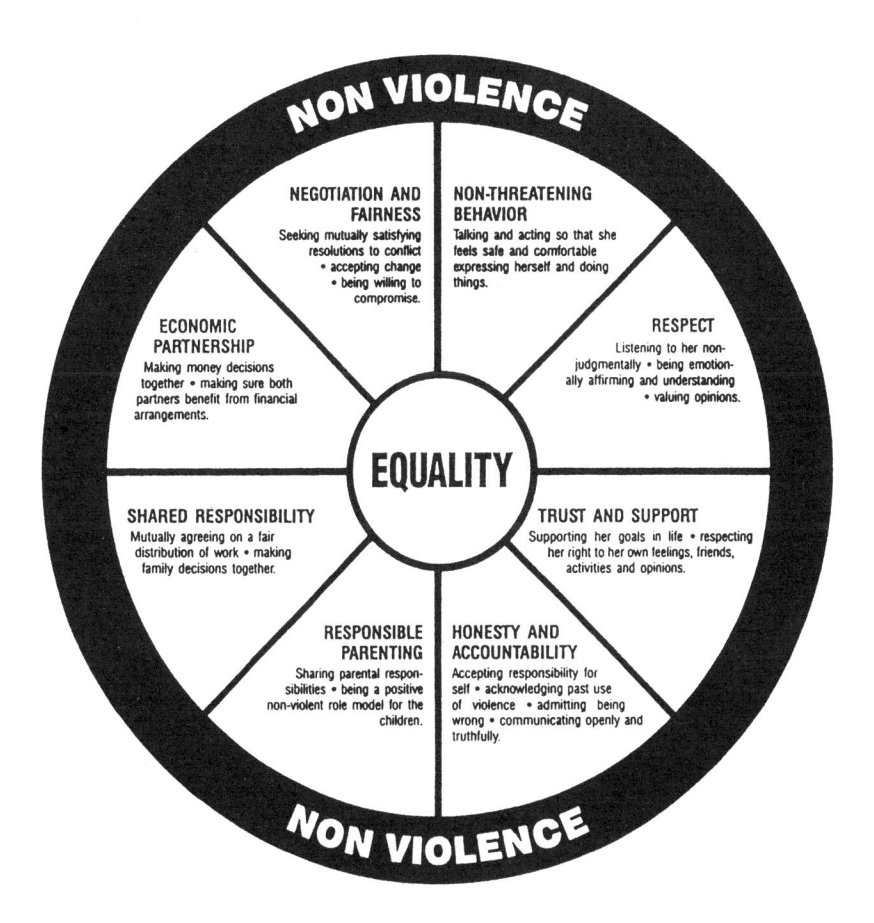

Cultural Issues

Men who are violent to wives or partners seem to be living up to cultural prescriptions and expectations. In Western societies, men are violent because: 'the socialization of men encourages an ideology that teaches and affirms violence by men to women; further, the society we live in is made up of sexist social institutions, dominated by men, which support men's power and control over women, and our history, tradition and myths condone and support men's oppression of women.'[1] This account by two New Zealand men involved in devising programmes for stopping men's violence to women includes reference to Christian teaching on roles of men and women in marriage, and to Eve's temptation of Adam and the long tradition of victim blaming.

Men may use violence as a means of control in the home when they feel out of control elsewhere, at work, for example, as some of the instances already mentioned demonstrate. Society's understanding of masculinity demands that men feel in control. They may be unable to express their feelings in any way except anger. For one woman, her husband's violence and callousness began after they had lost a young son. He had shown no emotion, and was unable to grieve at all, but seemed to be taking all his feelings out on his wife. That, of course, does not excuse his violent behaviour, or that of others like him.

That many men see violence in a relationship as 'normal' is borne out by a survey by the Middlesex University Centre of Criminology of women and men in Islington, published in 1994. This found: nearly 2 out of 3 men admit they would use violence on their wives or partners in conflict situations; 1 in 5 said they would react violently if their expectations over work or childcare were not being met; only 37% of men questioned said they would never use violence.

There has been much debate about whether domestic violence is more prevalent in certain cultures or classes. It is sometimes assumed it is more prevalent in working class families, but middle class women are less likely to report it, or to use public agencies and women's refuges. The 1989 Home Office report already cited concludes that domestic violence occurs in all classes and communities.

There is no evidence that Asian or Black women are more likely to experience domestic violence, but men may invoke religious or cultural orthodoxies as excuses to beat or coerce them. An Asian woman in Britain may find it more difficult to speak out about violence, or escape it. If a woman goes against the prescribed roles of her culture, she is seen to have shamed the honour of her family and her community, and is thus treated as an outcast.

Practical Responses

Where do women turn for help? Most women will turn first to family and friends. They may then approach police, GP, solicitor and housing

---

[1] McMaster & Swain, p 70.

department, and perhaps seek support and advice through voluntary agencies such as Samaritans, Citizens' Advice Bureau, Relate and Women's Aid. A study by WAFE in 1981 found that about 11% of women contact a minister or priest.

Often women do not readily find the help they need. A Parliamentary Committee report was published in 1975, establishing violence to women in their homes as a social problem. Since then, as a result of the campaigning efforts of the Women's Aid movement, there has been some legislation—four Acts concerned with domestic violence—and a Home Office Research Study in 1989. This concluded that domestic violence is a large problem, which is partially condoned by society and by the various agencies which might be expected to help, and suggested various changes.

In 1992 a Report by Victim Support of an Inter-Agency Working Party was issued, giving detailed recommendation on how to reduce domestic violence and to aid those who suffer from it.

In the last few years there have been some improvements. A 1987 policy change and 1990 Home Office circular have resulted in police being more likely to intervene. In the Metropolitan police, some stations have started a pro-arrest policy for common assault in domestic situations. Some forces have set up Domestic Violence Units with specially trained officers. In 1993 some schemes were launched to provide women at risk with telephone alarm systems. However, some women feel that little has changed, and that police are still trying to reconcile husbands and wives rather than act on an assault.

If a man is arrested, the normal practice is for the police to charge the offender and the case then goes to the Crown Prosecution Service. Often men who are arrested have the charges dropped, and few of the men convicted of assaulting their wives are imprisoned.

Most women seek medical help at least once, though shame and fear often prevents them going unless the injuries are severe. Some women are embarrassed to speak to a doctor, or afraid that their partner may find out. Many doctors are more aware and ready to pick up signs of violence and to be supportive. However, I heard of one GP who suggested to a woman suffering badly from the memory of being nearly killed by her partner that she did not need counselling, and that the best way to get over it was to find another relationship!

Many women turn to a solicitor, and there are now solicitors who have expertise in dealing with domestic violence cases, and can advise on what the law can do. Where a woman wants an attacker excluded from the house, a solicitor can get an Ouster Order, which forces the man to move out within 72 hours and is attached to an injunction to protect her and her children from physical harm. It is possible for a woman to seek an injunction without going for a divorce.

If a woman leaves her home because of domestic violence, the local housing department has a duty to re-house her if she is homeless and in priority need. If she wants to move away from her home area because she is afraid, she has the right to apply to another housing authority.

The most valuable help for most women comes from Women's Aid. The WAFE National Office provides information and resources, co-ordinates the lobbying, advocacy and training role of Women's Aid and runs the National Women's Aid Helpline, which gives advice and information. Local Women's Aid projects vary in their services and resources, but provide advice and support as well as emergency and temporary accommodation. The Helpline or local Women's Aid workers can help women think through what to do, and where to go if they want to get out of a violent relationship. Women's Aid resources and coordinates refuge provision; there are currently 200 refuges in England. There are some independent refuges, a few run by local authorities, and some catering for ethnic minority women.

There are separate linked organisations in Wales, Scotland and Northern Ireland which operate in a similar way.

Refuges provide a safe place to go to, if necessary at short notice. They have confidential addresses (and good security) for obvious reasons, but their phone numbers are available from Women's Aid, or local CABs, social services, Samaritans, Police, etc. They can be a place for a very short stay, or longer, while a women finds somewhere else to live, for example. Any woman experiencing any form of domestic violence is welcome, and any children. Refuge workers and the other women help with legal action, rehousing, welfare rights, and matters like children's schooling. During 1990 refuges provided shelter for 30,000 women and children.

3
'Battered into Submission'?

Theological Issues

'Each time your husband hits you just think of it as an opportunity to be a little closer to Jesus and the angels.'[1]

As I have already hinted, the predominating sociological theories include the church in their analysis of a society which sanctions or even contributes to men's violence against women. In fact, in nearly all the literature I have

---

1   A Borrowdale, 1991, *Distorted Images*, p 104, quoting an American pastor.

surveyed, Christian and secular, the claim is the same: 'The seeds of violence against women and children are embedded in the theology and teachings of the Church'.[1] Secular literature refers to patriarchy and unequal roles in marriage or specifically to scriptural injunctions; Christian writing refers more specifically to the origins of these. 'Church structures reinforce the subordination of women and, therefore, foster an environment in which domestic violence can occur.'[2] Perhaps the most stark conclusion comes from American Lutheran Joy Bussert, quoted by Anne Borrowdale: 'If submission continues to be the "theory", then battering will inevitably continue to be the "practice"'.[3] Other writing comes to similar conclusions.

It is in some ways not surprising that the US anti-feminist backlash includes opposition to women's refuges alongside a campaign to keep women in the home, bringing up children. Such accusations challenge traditional Christian teaching on marriage and on the roles of men and women in marriage (and outside it), and are extremely threatening, perhaps most so for evangelicals, for whom passages such as Ephesians 5:21- 6:9 have been fundamental. Some Christians seem to pass over 5:21 ('Be subject to one another...'), 5:25 and 6:4, while maintaining that whatever else happens, women must submit.

On the other hand, evangelical Christianity has been cited as one of the intellectual traditions which has shaped the nature of feminism in Britain and the USA. In the nineteenth century most women's rights leaders were products of evangelical backgrounds. Their understanding of the Bible's radical equality of the sexes gave the impetus to work for change in society. Evangelicals in the last two centuries were often the first to seek justice for the oppressed. Might not they be expected to do the same today?

Interpreting the Bible

Going back to the beginning of Genesis, it seems that the story of equality in creation and image in chapter 1 has not been as influential in most people's thinking as the apparently different chapter 2. According to some interpreters of Genesis 2, man was created first and superior. Woman was created second, to serve his needs. Furthermore, the image of Eve as the temptress in Genesis 3 has led to a tendency to see women as somehow 'causing' violence.

Some who write about domestic violence are tempted, not surprisingly, to demand an end to the power of such Christian 'myths'. But a few scholars assert that the Bible does not contradict itself, and that Christianity is not inherently patriarchal; rather, our interpretation (e.g. of *ezer* in Genesis 2:18

---

1 R Fitzmaurice, 1991, *A Sin and a Crime*, Wellington: Wellington Archdiocesan Catholic Commission for Justice, Peace and Development, p 2.
2 Committee on Women in Church and Society, (c 1988), *Domestic Violence: A Problem for the Church within Society*, Presbyterian Church of New Zealand, p 7.
3 Borrowdale, p 104.

as 'helper', with connotations of inferiority) has sometimes been at fault.

Further on into the Old Testament, there seems further fuel for those who would discard the Bible. Women appear as mothers, wives, concubines and harlots, and as the victims of outrageous acts of violence (with rare exceptions, such as Jael killing Sisera in Judges 4). There is no space here to discuss these in detail. But some interpreters have concluded that because such actions are not condemned, the OT (and God?) is anti-women. One might be reminded that the first two chapters of Genesis are about what God intended, and the rest of the Bible about what went wrong! If patriarchy, and domination of women by men is a consequence of the Fall, one would expect women to have been exploited.

To find what a restored humanity might look like one needs to look at Jesus. As many theologians have recently noted, Jesus had a revolutionary attitude towards women, challenging existing stereotypes, and affirming women as people and disciples, for example in his dealings with the Samaritan woman at the well in John 4, or Martha and Mary in Luke 10.

Jesus also stands in stark contrast to the contemporary 'ideology of men', an ideology of biological and intellectual superiority, control, competition, success, and lack of emotional expression, and is a radical challenge to it. Has some of this ideology seeped into the church? Or has the church failed to challenge it in the world? Does Jesus call men to control, competition and success? Or could it be, as Roy McCloughry suggests, that 'Real men lay down their lives for other people. Real men move from power to love,' reversing the priorities of masculinity.[1] Jesus served, wept, and sacrificed. He called his followers (of both sexes) to do the same.

Argument continues to rage about Ephesians 5. What is 'submission'? Who is to submit? Men have been taught that wives are to submit—and often that women are inferior to them, too. Wives have been taught to submit to husbands—even if they beat them. 'He [a Christian counsellor] very strongly emphasised that I am to obey my husband despite the violence because I'm really obeying God when I do this, and I need to die to self and see Christ as my all.'[2] While there is increasing conviction among evangelicals that submission is meant to be mutual, many churches continue to teach a hierarchical model of marriage. One American pastor teaches that a wife's submission to her husband guarantees a good relationship, and another that women should submit even if they suffer; following Jesus means suffering for righteousness' sake.[3] These are American examples, but many of the books on marriage read by British Christians originate in the USA.

---

[1] R McCloughry, 1992, *Men and Masculinity*, London: Hodder, p 77.
[2] Alsdurf & Alsdurf, pp 18-19.
[3] Ibid., p 78, 81-2

Church History and Tradition

The hierarchical model is enshrined in church history. Early church writers often saw women as inferior to men, Eve responsible for the Fall, all women as temptresses, and so on. A fifteenth century church Rule for Marriage directed a husband to beat his wife, if 'of a servile disposition', out of 'charity and concern for her soul',[1] and I have already quoted other similar examples.

The Reformation led to greater sanctification of marriage, which in turn resulted in greater authority for husbands. While wife-beating was discouraged, its practice was widespread. The emphasis on the individual did balance this to some extent, and evangelicals were forerunners of feminism in the eighteenth and nineteenth centuries. But also in the nineteenth century the Clapham Sect promoted the cult of womanhood in which male dominance and female submission were systematically elevated as cardinal Christian virtues. The same would be true today, in many churches. And this model persist in society too.

It must also be noted that the Anglican marriage service has only recently (1980) placed the main stress in marriage on mutual comfort and help. Previously, marriage was seen in terms of clear roles; the wife was to submit and obey. The 1928 Prayer Book placed emphasis on the woman as the submissive partner, enjoined to obey and depend on her husband.

But recent books on marriage perpetuate old myths and stereotypes. One book on marriage counselling by an influential author implies that if there is violence in the marriage the wife's behaviour may be to blame, she may enjoy violence in a masochistic way, or she may have grown up amid violence and not know any different. The husband's violence is attributed to immaturity or dependency, and external circumstances such as alcohol, illness, or sniping and flirtatious behaviour by the woman in public.

It does seem that a simplistic understanding of Scripture, overlaid with teaching of some dualist-influenced Church Fathers (associating men with reason and 'good', and women with the body and 'evil') has been partly responsible for creating a climate in which domestic violence could be condoned. The Alsdurfs quote statistics on the correlation of wife beating and unequal roles in marriage. One study found the rate of wife beating in couples where the husband dominated was 3 times greater than for egalitarian couples, and this has been confirmed by other studies.[2]

The Church Today

One refuge worker told me of a reactionary Christian group which, she said, quoted the Bible on male and female roles, and said it was OK for a

---

1   Quoted by Committee on Women in Church and Society, p 12.
2   Alsdurf & Alsdurf, p 86.

husband to chastise his wife. This particular refuge had a good relationship with the local Anglican church. But the worker told me that they had problems with local ministers wanting to come to the refuge and put pressure on women to go back home. They would remind the women of their marriage vows. Or they would suggest to the woman that, 'You're not praying enough'. Thus the guilt of such women was compounded, and they saw themselves as bad Christians as well as bad wives. A woman involved with another refuge told me that refuge workers there were very suspicious of the church—perhaps with good reason! Another said the judgmental attitude of the church made volunteer work in a refuge difficult for her. Refuge workers had been abused over the telephone by church ministers who had sided with the men involved and called the refuge on their behalf.

A conference in 1991 organised by the Network of Ecumenical Women in Scotland also produced examples of Christian complicity in male violence, and failure to help women. Stories were told of pastors disbelieving or blaming women, women counselled to return to their husbands and submit to them, and women who were scared to share their problems within the church, for fear of judgment and rejection.

The record and reputation of the church is not good. The manager of one refuge told me, 'People see us as a divorce agency'. Certainly the church seems to. But should some evangelical ministers be so obsessed with the sanctity of marriage and a horror of divorce that they send women back to the violence? There are, in any case, other options besides divorce for a women who goes temporarily to a refuge. And in a world where decisions are not always simple, in some cases divorce may be the lesser of two evils.

One writer compares wife battering to adultery in terms of marital breakdown. He concludes that one can use the word *porneia*, violation of one's partner, in the context of domestic violence, and that the degree of violation in wife battering may surpass that in adultery. Hence divorce as last resort in the case of violence is justified in the light of the exception clause in Matthew 19:9.[1]

As Kenneth Petersen concludes, 'The evangelical church may then, by means of its treatment of and attitude towards women, contribute to the climate in which domestic violence is tolerated or even allowed to flourish'.[2] If this is so, then the church has some work to do, for the sake of women, for the sake of men, for the sake of the gospel.

The church has recently done some re-thinking with regard to women in leadership. Many of the same issues affect attitudes to domestic violence. And in a similar way, just because a certain way of thinking is enshrined by centuries of church tradition, does not mean that it is necessarily right. We

---

[1] G P Liaboe, 1985, 'The Place of Wife Battering in Considering Divorce', *Journal of Psychology & Theology*, Vol 13 No 2, p 129-138.
[2] K Petersen, 'Wife Abuse: the Silent Church', *Christianity Today*, Nov 25th 1983, p 26.

need to look again at Scripture, at the whole of it, and the ways in which it has been abused, so that we can uphold the Bible as the word of God, and teach and preach it correctly and with integrity.

A deacon who has been involved with her local refuge told me how the women she encountered had been taught, implicitly or explicitly, that violence is their lot, that they deserve it, and their partner has rights over them. She felt that the church needs to be teaching the opposite, instead of perpetuating such ideas. She had found herself working against the verbal and other forms of abuse in the church as well as the abuse of women in their homes.

'If we participate in the institutionalized abuse of women...how much is our religion worth?'[1] We claim to have good news. We all sin, but in Jesus we find forgiveness. We need to take that message to all involved in the cycle of violence, together with the message that our God is the God of the oppressed, a God who hates injustice.

Women who have been victims of violence may ask, where is God? God is present in suffering. God protests against suffering which is an offence to love. 'If we are to learn how to protest against suffering and to change the conditions that cause it, we must first simply be present (as God is present) to those who are the victims.'[2]

4
Loosing the Chains of Injustice

'How long, O Lord, must I call for help,
but you do not listen?' (Habakkuk 1:2)

'Who will stand against the violence?...
Who will build for love a home?' (Graham Kendrick)

Pastoral Responses

Anne Borrowdale, one of the few British Christians who have written about domestic violence suggests: 'Our response to this kind of sin should include righteous anger, advocacy for the victim, and holding the offender legally and spiritually accountable.'[3]

---

1 Donald Cole, quoted Petersen, p 25.
2 P Fiddes, 1989, *Past Event and Present Salvation*, London: DLT, p 218.
3 Borrowdale, p 120.

Women who have experienced violence need most of all to be listened to. A woman may have been beaten many times before she will go to a stranger for help, without knowing what kind of reaction she will get. Will the vicar listen to her? Will he say, 'How can I help?' or will he say, 'Marriage is sacred and for life'?

Believe the woman—and let her know this. Let her go at her own pace, and ask open and unthreatening questions. Find out what has been happening and what she wants—to talk things through, or practical help. Women in immediate danger may need a safe place to go to—may even need help to 'escape'. The manager of a Christian crisis centre tells of how he once arranged for a woman's children to be collected from school, then picked up her, and her possessions which had been put outside her house in black rubbish bags, and drove them all to a refuge a safe distance away from her violent partner.

The woman may be concerned about practical issues: legal, medical, housing, her children (Are they witnessing the violence? Are they safe?). The local refuge or WAFE National Helpline may be the best source of information.

Feelings may include shame and guilt, anger, strong emotions, much hurt and pain—but she may also say, 'But he's not really violent...he only punched me/kicked me/pushed me downstairs' or whatever, and need reassurance that you take it seriously. As with any trauma, feelings may be expressed or repressed. I spoke to one woman who had done such a good job of repressing her feelings and appearing to cope that even her friends did not think the problem too serious; but when she was encouraged to talk the tears started to come.

A woman who has suffered, perhaps for a number of years, will take time to recover her self-esteem. She may have argued to herself, I must be bad if I deserve this, or she may have been subjected to verbal abuse, humiliation and put-downs. 'After a while you start to believe you're a whore, or sick, or whatever....' As many women in the church already lack self-esteem, Christians may suffer more in this respect than non-Christians.

If she has a faith she may be angry with God, feel let down that he has allowed violence to occur. She needs to know that it is all right to be angry with God, to use the words of the psalms which cry out to God. Then she may slowly come to see God as one who is on the side of the oppressed and humiliated, and find security in God.

Women who have been hurt by men may find it hard to look to a male God. Exclusively male imagery for God reinforces male power and a hierarchical understanding of creation. Christians seeking to help women need special sensitivity in speaking of God.

Do not expect to counsel the couple together. The woman needs to be protected, even if ultimately there is a possibility of reconciliation.

The other main pitfall to avoid is expecting the woman to forgive too soon. She may need assuring that righteous anger is OK. It is all right to be angry—but not to let the sun go down on it; it is unhealthy to stay angry. She should not be told how noble it is to suffer, or that it is woman's lot! Forgiveness may come later, but first the guilt of the man needs to be acknowledged and feelings worked through. And forgiveness does not necessarily mean going back, but the woman dealing with her own feelings towards the man who has abused her.

It will all take time, and healing may come through a variety of counselling approaches.

Women need to be accepted in the church community, which should be a place which demonstrates God's love and acceptance. I recently heard of a Christian who had been beaten by her husband and was then rejected by some of her Christian friends when she would not go back to him.

Women who have experienced violence need to see the God who clothed himself in frail humanity, to see Jesus who wept at his friend's death and did not isolate himself from human suffering. Such a God weeps with them at the effects of the evil of our world. We may hope and pray that those who suffer may see the cross as a sign of God's suffering with us in Christ, and the hope of resurrection. As we share in the suffering of those we encounter, they may find for themselves the God of all comfort.

Women who are black or Asian, living in a white society, may be especially isolated and find it even harder to get to the point of seeking help. A Christian from a Middle Eastern country went for help to a church-based advice centre when her husband, temporarily working as a doctor in Britain, beat her up. It had become so bad that she had packed her bags and walked out. She had telephoned her father but he would not let her return home to the family because of the shame if anyone in his community knew about it.

What of the man? He needs to be listened to as well, if he will talk. He may deny being violent, or belittle it. He may try to intimidate or threaten anyone who is aware of his violence.

But what really happened? If he has been violent, he needs to be held responsible for his actions, the law may need be allowed to take its course, and if he is a Christian, perhaps some kind of church discipline is appropriate. For some, the threat of prison may be a deterrent, or enough to shock a man into being prepared to think through and change his patterns of behaviour.

There is currently some debate in secular circles about male violence. Can men change? Do they want to change? Can they be made to? Most people in the refuge movement are sceptical about whether men's programmes can work; only changing the structures, and expectations of relationships will be effective. Only a handful of men have embarked willingly on men's programmes. However, I know of one man who telephoned the Women's Aid helpline seeking help for himself, because he had identified his violence as a problem through reading a magazine article; some men may be open to change.

Little has been done in Britain on work with men who are violent in the home, but it is more advanced in the USA and Canada, and the book by Hague and Malos describes five models of treatment programmes. It is too early to tell how successful they are. In Britain a few projects have been set up, some for voluntary self-referral and some which run court-ordered programmes. The Everyman Centre in Brixton offers individual counselling and group work, and runs a phone line, and there are a number of groups called Men Overcoming Violence (MOVE) around the country.

This is one area in which the church might have a voice. Sometimes the Church has seemed to have simplistic answers, and that needs to be avoided, but if domestic violence is seen as sin, there must always be room for change. Some men do not want to change. But for those who can acknowledge their past behaviour as offence against God and against their partner, there is always hope.

Counselling needs to address the motivation of violence. How does he expect to treat and relate to women? Is there a pattern to his behaviour? Are there family influences? How can he break his pattern of attitudes and behaviour? Can remorse turn to real repentance? Even if there seems a new attitude, regret and respite may just be part of a cycle of abuse. The work of reconciliation cannot begin until the man who has been violent repents, and for a woman to regain trust after it is been shattered will take time.

Anger management and similar programmes may have some success. But it will take more than anger management programmes and counselling to change years of evil habits. If a man is seriously sorry and wants to change, the Holy Spirit is able to break the power of evil and bring freedom, and, though it may take a long time, even situations which seem impossible can be changed.

Challenges for the Church

The church in Britain lags behind other churches when it comes to responses to domestic violence. In New Zealand, for example, a vicar in one parish identified domestic violence as one of the key social problems in his area. He developed a ministry of healing and empowering people caught in the cycle of violence.

In Canada, a special kit, 'Family Violence in a Patriarchal Culture: a challenge to our way of living', has been developed to help church officials and churchgoers better understand how abuse flourishes within a pattern of values and beliefs.

In Britain, Christians are beginning to act. In 1992 the Institute for the Study of Christianity and Sexuality organised a conference on 'Sexual Violence, Harassment and Abuse of Women in the Christian Community'. England has at least one Christian-based refuge, a church-based self-help group for men wanting to overcome violence, and a Church Urban Fund project.

Other Christians have been involved in their local refuges, usually only possible for women, as men are generally excluded. This can be an important if demanding area of service. One refuge worker told me that all the volunteers in her refuge were women who had experienced violence themselves, because only they were able to survive the stress and violence they had to encounter. As I have already suggested, women working in a refuge may be suspicious of Christians, and it is important that the church is seen as unconditionally welcoming, but there are opportunities for those who are trained and aware. Other ways in which churches might help a local refuge could be with money, clothing, furniture, or Christmas presents.

As the public profile of domestic violence has risen recently, and more and more women seek help, there is particular need for ongoing support for women experiencing violence but not wanting or ready to leave the relationship, for self-help groups and for counselling. These may provide opportunities for Christians to be involved, showing Christ's love.

The following points draw on the example set by churches overseas, the work of individual Christians, and the implications of this booklet.

1. The church needs to recognize its part in condoning or legitimating violence, however unwittingly, and admit its guilt. Repentance may be called for.
2. The church should also play its part in teaching that domestic violence is sin, which must be repented of on an individual level before reconciliation with God and with the victim of violence can occur.
3. It must recognise that domestic violence is a serious problem, occurring in church families as well as in wider society. And it must stop.
4. Church leaders and members need to make themselves better informed about the practical, pastoral and theological issues. Domestic violence and how to respond to it should be preached and taught about in churches.
5. Violence is often evident prior to marriage. Clergy have a unique role in helping to prevent violence by raising it as an issue during marriage preparation, and discussing honest communication and male-female roles. Often men have been taught to be aggressive, and women passive and submissive.
6. Churches should support and encourage those who protect and seek to help battered women.
7. Church leaders should challenge the prevailing unbiblical 'ideology of men' and instead promote a new model of what it means to be a man, based on Jesus. Male leaders need to be aware of their own example, and how they use power.

8. Churches and their leaders should be aware that the issues around family violence are complex. They must beware of simplistic answers, and aware that they can learn much from professional workers in secular organisations.
9. Clergy and others need to stop blaming the victim. Those who counsel must balance the upholding of a marriage relationship with the rejection of violence within it. They must also beware of 'cheap grace' for the men who are violent, and hold men responsible for their actions.
10. The church must address wider issues of sexism: language, discrimination at all levels, etc., and should encourage the leadership and ministry of women.
11. By taking domestic violence seriously and speaking out against it, the church must challenge society, and affirm that God is a God of justice and love, mercy and forgiveness. It can set an example by its openness to those who suffer, and by upholding a vision of a truly just and equal society, and a new humanity.
12. The gospel must be presented as good news for those who are violent and those who suffer violence alike. There must be hope for forgiveness, change and reconciliation in many situations, but an acknowledgement that this will never be easy and may not always be possible.

The prophet Ezekiel speaks God's warning and promise:
> 'You have not strengthened the weak or healed the sick or bound up the injured...They will know that I am the Lord, when I break the bars of their yoke and rescue them from the hands of those who enslaved them...They will live in safety, and no-one will make them afraid.' (Ezekiel 34:4, 27-28)

FURTHER READING

James Alsdurf & Phyllis Alsdurf, 1990, *Battered into Submission*, Crowborough: Highland Books.

Anne Borrowdale, 1991, *Distorted Images*, London: SPCK.

Aruna Gnanadason, 1993, *No Longer a Secret, The church and violence against women*, Geneva: WCC.

Gill Hague and Ellen Malos, 1993, *Domestic Violence, Action for change*, Cheltenham: New Clarion Press.

Sandra Horley, 1988, *Love and Pain: A Survival Handbook for Women*, London: Bedford Square Press.

Roy McCloughry, 1992, *Men and Masculinity*, London: Hodder.

Ginny NiCarthy, 1990, *Getting Free, A Handbook for Women in Abusive Situations*, London: Journeyman.

'It doesn't happen round here...' video introduction to WAFE, refuges and domestic violence, WAFE.

'Challenging Domestic Violence', training pack produced by Hammersmith and Fulham Community Safety Unit.

For further information: WAFE, PO Box 391, Bristol BS99 7WS tel. (0272) 633494. National Helpline: advice for women experiencing domestic violence, referral to local refuges: (0272) 633542. Everyman Centre: 071 793 0255; helpline for men: 071 793 0155.